Grieving

Through a Magical Celebration of Life

The New Normal

GUY MARINI

Grieving Through A Magical Celebration of Life: The New Normal

Copyright © 2022 Guy Marini

Produced and printed by Stillwater River Publications.

Visit our website at
www.StillwaterPress.com
for more information.

First Stillwater River Publications Edition

ISBN: 978-1-958217-77-1 *(paperback)*
ISBN: 978-1-958217-81-8 *(hardback)*

Names: Marini, Guy, author. | Marini, Guy. Ring the bell for our M.L.
Title: Grieving through a magical celebration of life : the new normal / Guy Marini.
Description: First Stillwater River Publications edition. | Pawtucket, RI, USA : Stillwater
  River Publications, [2023] | Contains children's story, Ring the bell for our M.L.
Identifiers: ISBN: 978-1-958217-77-1 (paperback) | 978-1-958217-81-8 (hardback)
Subjects: LCSH: Marini, Guy--Marriage. | Widowers--United States--Biography. |
  Wives--Death--Psychological aspects. | Grief. | Memorial rites and ceremonies. | LCGFT:
  Autobiographies.
Classification: LCC: HQ1058.5.U5 M37 2023 | DDC: 306.882092--dc23

1 2 3 4 5 6 7 8 9 10
Written by Guy Marini.
Contributing writers Matthew Marini,
Danielle Marini, and Erika Marini.
Celebration photographs selected by Nora Al Aleiwi.
Cover design by Matthew St. Jean.
Interior design by Elisha Gillette.
Published by Stillwater River Publications,
Pawtucket, RI, USA.

This book is dedicated to my beautiful and amazing
best friend and wife of forty years: Mary Lee (M.L.) Marini.
She had a certain magical charm that endeared her to all who were
fortunate enough to know her. She gave her family the gifts of love,
strength, and joy. When we walked into the home M.L. made for us,
we entered a sanctuary of caring and warmth that made us smile
even during the toughest of times.

Acknowledgments

This book came to life thanks to my grief counselor, Ms. Brenda Hartman. Ms. Hartman shone a light on the grieving process for me. I am very grateful to Brenda and to my friend, Dr. Tim Dukes, for introducing her to me.

- Lou Collignon
- Christie Cardillo Velezig
- Diana Ciociola
- Elaine Testa
- Joanie Bookbinder
- Judi Dill
- Judy Gagne

The other source of inspiration for this book came from my grief support group at Hope Hospice, Providence, Rhode Island. Thank you to our excellent and caring facilitators Ed Richard and Jamie Nero; and of course, my fellow grievers:

- Linda Casey
- Leah Joubert
- Mary Jo Gambardella
- Roger Clark
- Sharon Mansolillo
- Sue Lowell
- Ann Simonelli

Preface

The writing style of this book is, for lack of a better word, "choppy." It is part outline and part prose. When I sat down to write it, the words simply came out as they did. In a way, the story and the way it's written mirror the disjointed grieving process that I and so many others go through. It's up and down—two steps forward, three back, a couple sideways and you never know what will trigger a moment or a day full of pain.

There are times for smiles and laughing too as we move from the agony of loss to nostalgic ache for the loved one you lost. Who knows what the future holds as I experience this grief? I am two years removed from the day my M.L. passed. I still mourn her loss, love her, miss her and smile when I recall our life together.

So, please bear with the way it's written.

The book's intent is to share some ideas regarding how our traditional way of celebrating the loved ones we lose can be challenged in a positive manner. I took some time to provide some context as to how my family and I got "there."

What is "there"? There, for us, was a party—a life celebration over the traditional mourning ceremony for M.L. She asked us to have a celebration, a party as her remembrance. This is Part One of this work.

Part Two, the poetry I wrote for my M.L., is provided to build a picture for you of where our hearts were as we (M.L. and I) prepared for the loss of our earthly love.

These poems, for me, were the beginning; to see if I could share something with others that may help them if and when they go down this same road.

Part Three tells the story of how I came to write a children's book aimed at helping children deal with loss. With the help of Hope Hospice in Rhode Island, I am trying to assist children and teens (ages six to seventeen) cope with the passing of a loved one. The book, *Ring the Bell for Our M.L.*, is the basis of a workshop where I encourage and guide children to write a story about the loved one they lost.

PART ONE

*Can the New Normal for Grieving
Be Having a Magical Celebration of Life
vs. Traditional Grieving Norms?*

CHAPTER ONE

My Loss: Guy

Meet Mary Lee (M.L.) Marini

- Absolute love of my life
- High school sweethearts at sixteen
- I was instantly smitten: bright eyes... beautiful smile...husky voice...infectious laugh...generous heart...strong...beautiful...persistent...smart...tough
- We had nothing but each other. No means, no money
- We built a life together
- Three kids, (Matthew, Danielle, and Erika), a daughter-in-law (Melissa), two grandchildren (Ethan and Mackenzie)
- My M.L. had three labors in childbirth, all different: one lasted twenty hours, the next lasted two hours, and our youngest was born in two minutes. On that occasion...

She woke me at 12:05 a.m. on December 2, 1985 and told me it was time.

I leapt up, got the bag one prepares to go to the hospital, and attempted to put on her tights.

She said nope...not going to make it to the hospital. I said "Bullshit" and for the first time ever and since, I was attempting to put her leggings on while she was attempting to take them off.

Then she broke water, I lifted her into my arms to take her to the car...

AND

She looked at me with a look I had never seen before or since and she said, "PUT ME DOWN"

AND

I slowly did.

After that, I sprang into action like a superhero—calling the hospital, our midwife, the police, fire department, and 1-800-Oh My God (God was busy and couldn't come to the phone).

As I bounded back up the stairs, she had delivered Erika Leigh Marini, and

my M.L. was placing Erika on her chest.

My M.L. smiled at me, glowing with this beautiful little girl in her arms.

My M.L. delivered her all by herself.

Now that's strong...tough...and beautiful...

CHAPTER TWO

My Loss: Matt

My mom was someone who always supported me and encouraged me to be the most authentic version of myself. She saw what I felt passionately about and guided me as I explored those passions, cultivating my inner strength with constant support and acceptance. Her love gave me the confidence to trust in myself every day. She believed in me, and I truly feel that without her love and support, I wouldn't be who I am today. There isn't a day that goes by that I don't think of my mom and the love that she had for her son.

In these last few years, my mom battled cancer, until it ultimately consumed her body. However, during that fight, it never took her spirit—middle fingers up in the air the entire time. I remember one of the last times I spent with her, I hugged her. In fact, I squeezed her...I could feel her ribs. Years later, I can still feel her ribs. I remember that moment so clearly. When I released her from my arms, she smiled her big, bright smile and said, "I love you, my favorite son." I responded, "You don't have to say son, we all know the truth." We laughed. I loved making her laugh. I miss that laugh.

After she passed, the hardest part for me was seeing the loss through my children's eyes. Knowing I couldn't take that pain away...and even if I could, there wasn't room inside of me to take it on. Even in her passing, she man-

aged to make our family stronger, just like she wanted. Every day since, I've tried to continue strengthening our family, bringing us closer together, because I know that's what she truly wanted. That's why she wanted a celebration of life, rather than a traditional funeral; because she knew how it would bring people together, allowing them to grow closer while reinforcing their bond. She knew the healing power of a good party, and she loved a good party. Being in Virginia, hours away from home, I couldn't provide as much help with the planning as I would have liked, but watching my father and sisters work towards my mom's celebration of life was inspiring. To see their outpouring of love to create something so beautiful and beyond comprehension was amazing. Their dedication was a true testament to the love my mom nourished.

The party, itself, was perfect. A crisp New England night in November. The location was surrounded by a sense of freshness only nature can provide; a sense of peace and tranquility in the air. You walked in through great, big, inviting doors and were immediately surrounded by warmth and love; it enveloped you. Bushels of hydrangeas and roses painted the room. People congregated around food and drinks as a sense of comfort formed in the room. Everyone somberly gathered, not knowing what to expect. Images of my mom, her artwork, and others' artwork could be seen along a large banquet

table memorializing my mom. Oh, and booze. All the elements of a Mary Marini party. The room felt packed but wasn't. Love filled the air and any void we felt was filled with music. It was beautiful.

As the celebration of my mom's life started, people began to see the direction in which it was heading. Grief wasn't the guest of honor. My mom was, her life was, and what she had left behind. Her spirit. Her love for life. Her love for her family. A video featured front and center displayed memories of her life, events, and family and friends. Everyone in attendance held witness to her life; her ups, and her downs. There were tears and laughter, happiness and sadness. The tragedy of what was lost, but also the beauty of what was built.

In my mind, this celebration allowed others to view my mom beyond her death. It gave everyone perspective on how she lived and how she positively affected each person's life. It gave her humanity in death. This celebration was an ability to showcase my mom's life from multiple perceptions, cast in a light beyond sadness. People saw joy and happiness. As the night progressed, you could feel something. Her presence? Collective healing? I couldn't tell you...but a warmth was there. It was a powerfully mystical experience fueled by love.

Grief is an essential component when processing the loss of a loved one, but in our current society, it appears to be our only recourse. Ceremonial norms, like wakes or funerals, seem to be our only way in honoring the passing of

a loved one. To me, they are one-dimensional. The people attending these events merely get a flat representation of that person's life: their passing. While it is important and necessary to feel that pain, there seems to be something missing. After my mom's celebration of life, we found what was missing. What our family experienced together filled us up. It helped balance the pain of her loss. It made us feel like everyone there, witness to her life outside of her death, will never let us forget all that she was, everything that she embodied. The love seen that night reassured our friends and family that those who lived and loved like her will forever be unforgettable. It taught me that people will remember. People will heal.

CHAPTER THREE

My Loss: Danielle

What will heaven be like? A question that runs through my head every day. My mom asked me this near the end of her life.

My response: "I don't really know but I do know it'll be the most beautiful place you've ever seen."

A smile from my mom and then more silence as we knew time was passing by.

Losing a parent, which many of us have experienced, is a gut-wrenching experience.

I will say that I connected with my mom more than I'd ever had in my life while she was in the process of dying.

Honesty, Vulnerability, Safe, and Blessed, are a few of the words that come to my mind when I think about our conversations.

The conversations were real. It could be scary sometimes but it always felt good to be so open. I asked her all the things. I asked if she was scared. I asked anything that came to my heart. She was strong, compassionate, and brutally honest with her take on things. I smile thinking back on it. I am blessed for having that time with my mom. I have no regrets and I said everything I wanted to say. When she died, I knew she loved me and in return, she knew she was loved.

I miss her like crazy every day. It never goes away. Finding the silver lining in my mom's passing has been a saving grace.

I watched her live a happy authentic life and I watched her leave this life to experience something more beautiful than she's ever seen.

CHAPTER FOUR

My Loss: Erika

The loss of my mother, Mary Lee, holds an enormous impact in my life. Greater than any words used in this essay. The grief has been anything but linear. The loss is too big to hold at times. In the first few months that followed my mother's death, joy seemed so far away. So distant. The crack in my heart was deepening. The echo of her laugh, her smile, her grace, spirit, and unconditional love are what moved me physically through each day. It was not until we were able to celebrate her life that I finally felt my heart crack wide open, fill with joy and awe in the strange beauty of loss. My heart broke wide open. Holding her spirit, honoring her legacy, and finding glimmers of sparkle in the eyes of family and friends is what propelled me to understanding that love through loss is a profound feeling. A feeling that has catapulted me into understanding life's fragility, which guides me into living a more curious life filled with love and compassion. I will carry her with me; she is my Mary Lee.

CHAPTER FIVE

Her Illness and Path Through

My M.L. was diagnosed with multiple sclerosis at forty-five. COPD by the time she was fifty-five and finally cancer at sixty-one.

She was in a wheelchair for about nine years.

She was hospitalized twice with pneumonia within four months and on oxygen 24/7 for seven years.

During cancer, she endured thirty-three radiation treatments and chemotherapy.

She never lost her engaging, bright spirit. There was no darkness in her and she would not allow "any Death Talk" as she progressively got weaker.

As I walked with her during this journey, I saw many sick people. I found so many of those very ill people to be dark, depressed, and down. But not my M.L.—she was upbeat... smiling...dressed beautifully...hair done...lipstick....engaging....present.

She lit up every room I wheeled her into. She lifted me and those she came into contact with: doctors, nurses, nurse practitioners, administrative people, technicians, and other patients.

AND

There was always this moment with the medical profession—internists, pulmonologists, neurologists, oncologists, their staff— when they would stop, look at her and see the true M.L. "Oh, this one's different..."

My M.L. was bright, cheerful, and smiling to the very end. On the last night of her life, she was enjoying Tito's vodka with soda and two limes while eating crackers, cheese, fruit, and laughing with our daughter, Erika.

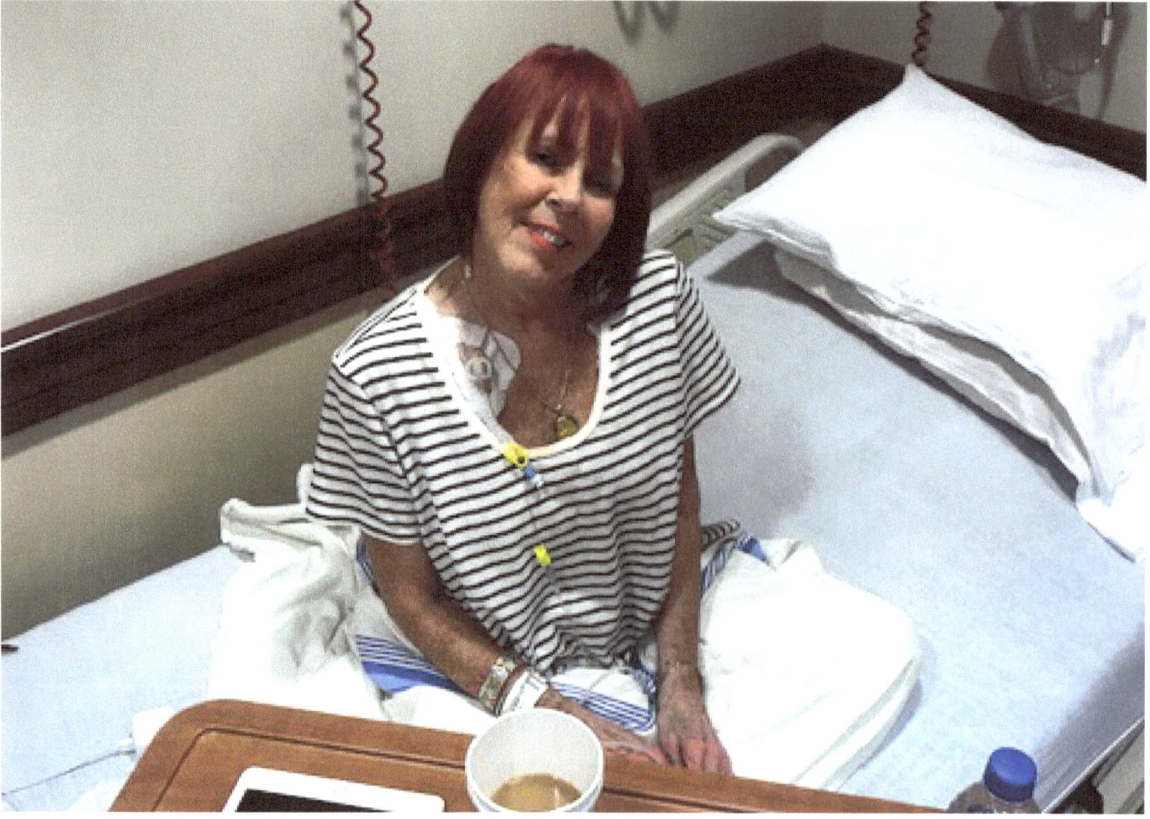

CHAPTER SIX

The Day She Died

She passed in the morning in that same bed where she delivered Erika. I was sitting next to her, holding her left hand. Erika was on her mom's other side holding her right hand. Our son, Matt, and his wife, Melissa, called from Virginia and were able to say goodbye to our M.L. The symmetry of life—the three of us together in that room...on that bed...where M.L. gave life to Erika...our M.L. passed on.

Strangely there was beauty in the moment

BUT

She didn't go willingly or easily.

Hospice came in and pronounced her time of death at approximately 9:30 a.m.

We're in shock...

Erika and I went downstairs and periodically went back and visited her. Our other daughter, Danielle, came and spent some time with her mother.

At noon, I spoke with my daughters. Our M.L. had made such a beautiful loving home for us. She was just so alive and spirited while making our home. Now, I thought it was time that we honor her wish and have her taken for cremation. I simply said, "I think she should go now." The three of us agreed.

I called the funeral home at 12:30 p.m.; they said they would be at our home by 1:00 p.m., at the very latest. I called them around 1:45 p.m.; they said they would be there "shortly." At 2:30 p.m., they called me to say that the vehicle had a flat tire and told me how sorry they were. At 3:00 p.m. they called and said "Mr. Marini, this wasn't just a flat, it was a major blowout. The two people in the vehicle can't fix it themselves and they are waiting for AAA."

At first, I was incredulous. Puzzled, I asked, "How long have you guys been in business?"

She answered, "My husband and I started the cremation/funeral home business forty years ago."

I then asked, "Has something like this ever happened before?"

She answered after a brief pause, "Nope. Never...I'm so sorry."

I ended the call and went to see my M.L. and said, "You really didn't want to go, did ya? My beautiful M.L., if you are going to come back to life can you do it now...please? I'll cancel the pickup."

They showed up to pick up M.L. at 4:30 p.m. Three and a half hours later than promised. She didn't go easily or willingly. I still wonder, *Can someone who passes have the ability to get a tire to disintegrate on a funeral home vehicle?* The answer was clear.

CHAPTER SEVEN

Those Last Three Years

- I left my job three years before she passed.
  - » Best thing I ever did. I was fortunate to have that flexibility
- Cared for her every day and night for three years.
- Our respect, admiration, and love grew.
- We helped each other, cried a little bit, I kissed her endlessly and it still wasn't enough. We laughed too...
- One time, I was taking her to an infusion clinic. I got her out of the car and into the wheelchair. However, I inadvertently knocked her wheelchair over with her in it. As I rushed to see if she was okay, she just looked at me and said, "You're shitting me, right...you gotta be shitting me." People who were there were appalled but she was okay. We laughed about it later. Honestly, she didn't laugh about it till much later...

I wouldn't trade those three years for anything. Ever.

I wrote some poems for her. I started writing some children's books to keep my brain going. I wrote two children's books about my M.L.

One is a "semi-fictional" account about how we met. The other is a book I wrote about her life as a grandmother (Nonna) and the adoration and love she bestowed on Ethan and Kenzie. The book is entitled *Ring the Bell for Our M.L.* and is intended to help children deal with the loss of a loved one.

The poems and book are reprinted here in this book. My M.L. gave me her never-ending encouragement in my writing and other endeavors; she always believed in me more than I believed in myself.

We walked together those last three years like we never ever walked before...we both knew where we were headed and prayed there was some way to alter the end of our story.

But there wasn't...

And then she passed...

And then we move into the next phase: the wake, funeral, a luncheon...

BUT

She had given me my instructions. She wanted a celebration...a party.

I asked her to define it for me, give me some direction please.

She said, "You'll figure it out, you know me." Further inquiries by me were met with, "No death talk, please."

She passed on February 13, 2020...and now we get hit with Covid and by early March we go into lockdown while having to figure out how to have a party for someone who passed, an innately sad event with a challenge to make it a tribute of some kind that reflects the sadness of the loss of her. And yet, we have to find a way to have some joy and laughs...and now that horrific pandemic too.

CHAPTER EIGHT

Our Ethnic Traditions [*]

Regarding the Loss of a Loved One

ITALIAN	**IRISH**
100% = Guy	100% = Mary Lee

ITALIAN	IRISH
☑ Wake	☑ Wake
☑ Open Casket	☑ Open Casket
☑ Lines of people	☑ Lines of people
☑ "Sorry for your loss"	☑ "Sorry for your loss"
☑ Tears	☑ Tears
☑ Attendees sitting, talking, laughing	☑ Attendees sitting, talking, laughing
☑ Funeral Mass	☑ Funeral Mass
☑ Collecting pictures/videos	☑ Collecting pictures/videos
☑ Pallbearers	☑ Pallbearers
☑ Limo with Casket	☑ Limo with Casket
☑ Eulogy	☑ Eulogy
☑ Pain	☑ Pain
☑ Entrance/Exit by Family	☑ Entrance/Exit by Family
☑ Graveyard	☑ Graveyard
☑ Flowers at Graveyard	☑ Flowers at Graveyard
☑ Lowering of Casket	☑ Lowering of Casket
☑ Lunch	☑ Lunch
☑ Drinking	☑ Drinking
☑ Drinking	☑ Drinking
☑ Drinking	☑ Drinking
	☑ Drinking

[*]   Things to do, what you experience, things that happen

- So M.L. was an Irish-American kid and I am an Italian-American kid. The table on page 13 shows just some of the things you need to do to organize a wake and funeral. In our cultures, this is expected to be done within a few days. There's a lot to do—it's not easy, it is what is traditional and expected.
- There's not much different between our ethnic groups; and yet the edge goes to the Irish regarding drinking but not by much
- Been to tons of wakes/funerals/luncheons and there is some comfort and closure to be had
- People don't know what to say...
  » Their well-intended words don't stay with you
  » How about this one: "The deceased looks good!!!"
- After experiencing the loss of my M.L. I realized just how pedestrian my comments to the affected families were when I attended a wake or funeral
- One experience at a wake always sticks out in my mind:
  » It was towards the end. People who hadn't seen each other for a while were talking, laughing, really enjoying themselves. I found myself looking at them and smiling. These people are enjoying a moment of camaraderie as they witness one of life's hardest events: the end of it. I turned and saw the family of the deceased: red-eyed, sad, and despondent still in line looking at all the laughing, happy people. It touched me, the contrast...it just didn't feel right...

My M.L. didn't want to go
- Laid out in a casket with someone picking out a dress, jewelry, etc. I can hear her saying, "Besides, who is going to do my hair and my makeup? Someone at a funeral home—not happening!"
- She didn't want us to go through the pain of that process and witness those who were laughing, and joking—not that those people were doing anything wrong; it was the cultural norm of our ethnic groups and the way wakes and funerals are traditionally done.

She wanted her life and her experiences in life celebrated. It was like my M.L. was saying, "Remember me and the fun we had, feel the loss yet show people the magic in my life and thank them for being part of it by throwing me, our family, and them a party."

CHAPTER NINE

Covid and its Impact on M.L.'s Celebration

- Started thinking about the celebration...
- Wrote down some ideas
- Started a eulogy...
  » Not easy...wrote three different versions and none of them were satisfactory to me. It couldn't capture what she meant to me and our family...
- I scheduled a place for the celebration at the end of April 2020, but Covid shut us down.
  » It shut us down in April 2020... then June of 2020...then October of 2020...
- Finally, as the Covid fog started to lift I tried to schedule the celebration and had to go out to November 2021 (twenty-one months after she passed). The backlog of delayed weddings caused by Covid prevented us from doing it any earlier.
- Covid was a blessing in disguise...
- We had time to grieve...
  » I found a wonderful grief counselor thanks to a very good friend
  » I joined an amazing support group ten months after M.L. passed—I needed help
  » I read...I listened to the grief counselor and members of my support group
  » My kids were there for me
  » My grandchildren talked to me about their Nonna
- I could not figure out or get to a proper eulogy. My adult children struggled with her passing. I was overwhelmed with her loss and my emotions around it.
  » When it came to a eulogy or remembrance, my daughter Danielle told me many times, "Dad, just tell the love story you two had."
  » Others in their chats with me regarding the loss of my M.L. would say things like, "You two had an epic love story"; "You two seemed so in love with each other." I heard this any number of times.

We met as young teenagers...became high school sweethearts...fell deeply in love and stayed together through all of life's challenges and triumphs. It felt too personal but I tried to tell our love story. I got something down on paper but knew I couldn't articulate it live in front of people.

Danielle directed me to a company that could produce a video with my words accompanied by pictures and music. It took me a while to gather the pictures, select the music, and finalize my words. Danielle and Erika helped me.

It came together one year after her death and I shared it on a Zoom call with my family, Katie (my sister-in-law), and her family. There were about ten of us. It felt right. If I was rushed into this remembrance by the norms defined by our ethnic groups and our culture at large it couldn't have and wouldn't have been the same. Covid forced me and my family into taking time to get an appropriate tribute for our M.L.

We now had nine months to finalize the celebration.

We were able to plan every detail:

- The food
- The drink
- Memory table
- A children's book and poem I had written as giveaways to the attendees
- Angel pins
- Flowers
- Balloons
- A couple of special dances

AND

- The atmosphere we wanted to create

It weighed on me and my family but the event was all we could have hoped for...

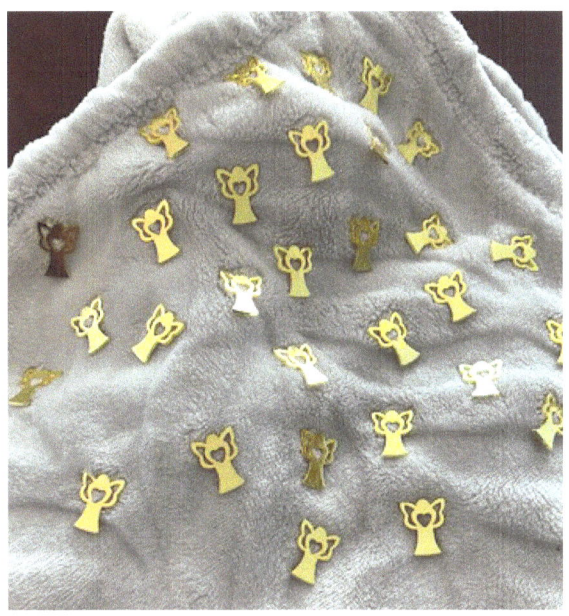

CHAPTER TEN

The Event

My M.L. loved to entertain...

The event was held at a local country club with a ballroom that seated up to 150 people comfortably. It's a hundred-plus-year-old place with a warm feel. It was where she would have wanted it.

ANGEL PINS

Let me tell you about the angel pins...

About ninety days before she passed, my M.L. reached out to her "angels" for help. I found some angel lapel pins; we started wearing them around the house and asked the hospice people and our visitors to wear them as well. When my M.L. opened her eyes every morning, I would attach the angel pin to her clothing.

She had this blanket, and every day she survived she would remove the angel pin from her clothing and place it on the blanket. There were about ninety pins on that blanket when she passed...

My grandchildren and my son, Matt, met every guest as they entered the event and handed everyone an angel pin for their lapel, dress, jacket....In that moment, there was a signal to the attendees that this event was something different from the norm.

ENTRANCEWAY

- As they entered, our guests were greeted by a beautiful picture of our M.L. accompanied by a lovely bouquet of blue and white flowers.
  - » Blue hydrangeas, white roses, blue and white astroemeria, baby's breath...her favorites.
- My daughters Erika and Danielle took and hung everyone's coats.

ENTERING THE BALLROOM

- I greeted everyone that came into the main entrance to the ballroom
- As they entered the ballroom, what they saw was an array of finger food at an appetizer station, an open bar, and a memory table.

MEMORY TABLE

- The memory table consisted of:
  - » Thirty individual framed pictures of our M.L.
  - » Our wedding album
  - » Some artwork that our M.L. had completed in the last few years of her life
  - » A wood-carved vase with a single red rose that was created by a cousin, Angelo Garofolo, that commemorated our fortieth anniversary.
  - » A painting called *Strength and Beauty* done by a very talented artist from Cape Cod who has done work for Marlo Thomas, Phil Donahue, Ted Kennedy, and others. Her name is Christine Cardillo Velesig. The painting shows our M.L. standing at the base of a lighthouse surrounded by beautiful flowers.
  - » A memory box where we asked people to share a thought/memory or our M.L.
  - » A children's book I had written called

Ring the Bell for our M.L. Again, it was written to help children understand loss. I also wrote several poems for my M.L.

» One was called *Passing and Beauty*. My determined M.L. had them all published in an online cancer journal called *Cancer Cure*

» *Passing and Beauty* was reprinted as a bookmark and placed inside the children's book. We invited our guests to take one if they wished; they were all gone by the end of the evening.

» And, yes, vases of blue and white flowers on the memory table.

THE DECOR

As our guests enjoyed passed hors d'oeuvres and a drink they gazed upon tables set up with white tablecloths, azure blue napkins with those beautiful blue and white flowers, and a blue balloon attached to each vase.

We set up tables of ten. The lady at the table whose birthday came closest to November 20 was instructed to take the flowers while the most senior gentleman at the table was asked to take the balloon when he left the event and release it to the sky.

SPEAKING PROGRAM/VIDEO

After an hour or so of socializing, we began a brief speaking program and showed the video of the love story between my M.L. and me.

My daughter Erika kicked off the event with a four-minute touching, sweet, funny, loving introduction that captured the essence of our M.L., focusing on the relationship between mother and daughter. It was composed and delivered brilliantly and genuinely. I then introduced the thirteen-and-a-half-minute video

simply asking our guests to focus on this radiant, magnetic woman that we were there to honor.

The video was personal, intimate, and authentic. I could not watch it...I had my head bowed sitting in my chair as it played. Occasionally I would raise my head to look at our guests; they seemed captivated by my M.L.'s video tribute.

I stood up after the video and toasted our guests and my M.L.

I thanked our guests for being there and honoring the love affair between M.L. and me. I shared that my M.L. and I wanted to honor the love affairs of our guests by inviting every couple to get up and dance to "Unforgettable" by Nat and Natalie Cole. The entire room, *every* couple, got up to dance.

Now came the challenging part in my mind. My M.L. wanted a party. She liked to dance even though she wasn't a great dancer (God forgive me for saying this), she loved to talk to people, tell stories and laugh...

After a genuine and authentic video, my daughter's amazing heartfelt introduction, the pictures, M.L.'s artwork, the angel pins, how were our guests going to react? Would they simply sit, have their dinner, chat and laugh while sitting at their tables? We knew there was a risk of that. And...so what? Well, it wasn't what our M.L. wanted. We so desired to deliver for her this night, her party, as a gift and tribute to her.

My kids and I spent the dinner hour going from table to table checking on our guests. It was clear from some of the people I interacted with in the weeks leading up to the celebration that most didn't know what to expect from this celebration of life, given the way our culture deals with death. It was clear to me that both sides of our families and friends were uneasy or a bit nervous, even slightly anxious, about what this celebration was going to be like. This was so understandable—generally, the collective

experience of all of our guests regarding loss was the traditional wake, funeral, and burial.

Our guests shared the following after dinner as people relaxed into the evening: "It was beautiful"; "The video, the music...Erika and you brought her back to life"; "I know it was a long illness and now I can see what it looked like"; "She seemed to handle it with such grace."

I took it all in and felt as though everyone was being polite, kind, and thoughtful.

And then it happened.

THE CONGA LINE

My M.L. loved a conga line...

The D.J. called for Erika to start a conga line. I heard it...I saw her start the line. Someone grabbed me and I had my back turned towards the dance floor. After a minute or two the person who grabbed me to chat said, "Hey, we're among the few not in the conga line."

As I turned, I saw approximately 110 of our 120 guests dancing in a conga line to the opening lyrics of Gloria Estefan's "Conga."

I stopped for a moment and simply smiled from ear to ear, so grateful to our guests, my M.L., my family, and Covid. I knew at that point we had done it.

We had delivered a gracious, loving, fun celebration for our M.L.

The rest of the night was fabulous as some of the younger folks entertained us with various dances I couldn't do—the Worm (what on earth?!). Everyone danced! Line dances, modified Rockette-style leg kicking, hugs all over the place, everyone laughing...

Thanks to all of you for being here to celebrate our M.L.

As the evening wound down, the night ended with "Time to Say Goodbye" by Andrea Bocelli and Sarah Brightman. After that, some left, yet a lot of people hung around to talk and be together.

One young man who had recently married into our family pulled me aside to say, "I didn't know M.L. but I think I know her now...what you guys did tonight was amazing."

Another gentleman told me, "The last eighteen months with my wife have been rough; I'm going to try to do better and be a better husband to her."

The videographer who handled all the technical details (i.e.: showing the video, etc.) also took some pictures and filmed part of the event. At the end of the evening, he shared "I've done a lot of these celebrations but none as beautifully done as this one."

I heard over and over again that:

- "Your M.L. is smiling down at you."
- "You guys did a superb job."

"The way we normally send someone off in our family is so sad—this is the way to do it."

We had the celebration for our M.L. that she would have wished for and it was better and more alive than I thought it would be.

AND

Something else happened in that room...

It was as if there was a collective reflection by many in that room, that this celebration, this tribute, was indeed a way to somehow grieve and celebrate the life of someone who passed.

If I heard it once, I heard it a hundred times: This event was "amazing." "What a tribute to M.L."

Finally, the event described was what my M.L. would have wanted; she would have LOVED the whole thing. Obviously, a celebration of life can be done any way that suits you and your loved ones.

In my case, it would have to be a bit lower

key. First, wait for sunny, mild weather, perhaps early to mid-September—always nice that time of year in Rhode Island. My preferred venue? The backyard.

Food...let's dive into some "prosciutto crudo," an Italian uncooked, unsmoked, and dry-cured ham. I do have one requirement however: a brand called Parma prosciutto—no substitutes, please. Next, let's slice up some sharp provolone. Now bring on some crusty Italian bread...some olives...some nice olive oil...

All of this followed by a nicely prepared tiramisu and a traditional Italian cake called zuppa inglese. I think our guests would enjoy drinking a traditional Italian chianti...

It would be nice to have an accordion player roam around and play requests. I encourage sing-alongs by the attendees (that's if anybody shows...).

Finally, wrap up the celebration with three songs: "God Bless America," "Arrivederci Roma," and "This Guy's In Love With You." The first is my favorite song about the USA. The second is a nod to my wonderful parents, Pasquale and Onelia Marini. The last is the song I listen to over and over again since I lost the love of my life: my M.L.

Yep, that celebration sounds about right for me.

COLLECTIVE EFFERVESCENCE

My children, grandchildren, and I returned to our home after M.L.'s celebration of life. We were relieved, happy, grateful, and emotionally spent.

It's unclear if any of us ate very much so we sat at our kitchen table, had some food, and talked.

The overriding theme and question we asked ourselves was this: "What happened in that ballroom tonight?" There was a feeling, a generosity of spirit, a collective embrace of what we tried to accomplish. We recognized the sadness of our loss yet we rejoiced and became more cognizant of our shared humanness...

The four of us were just sitting there trying to figure it out—just what did happen in that room the evening of M.L.'s celebration?

A few months later Erika called and simply said, "Google 'Collective Effervescence' and call me back."

Collective effervescence is a sociological concept identified by Emile Durkheim. According to Durkheim, a community or society may at times come together and simultaneously communicate the same thought and participate in some action. From a religious perspective, there are moments in life when a group of individuals that make up a society, if you will, comes together to perform a religious ritual.

Now, it doesn't have to be a religious ritual. A modern-day example of collective effervescence is at a soccer match. When a team scores a goal the crowd celebrates. This is simply a group of people doing the same thing at the same time. It's all spontaneous, so no one really knows it's going to happen.

In our case, our guests were invited to a celebration of life. Many who attended had never been to one, but they had been to tons of traditional wakes and funerals. So there was a sort of anxiety and curiosity amongst those who came.

As they saw our celebration of life unfold, I believe we sort of held the collective spirit of the room in a careful way. As the night went on, our guests became more comfortable. They opened their hearts to us.

Our guests experienced this "new" ritual, and they allowed themselves to partake in the celebration fully. It was beautiful.

Given my lack of knowledge of sociological matters, I find this idea of collective effervescence fascinating and I am convinced our 120 guests and my family experienced it.

Durkheim explains that collective effervescence is important because it allows society to recharge its batteries. Every society needs to reaffirm its moral unity through meetings, gatherings, rituals, ceremonies, or assemblies. He goes on to share that sometimes people experience "euphoria" in these moments.

A few months after M.L.'s celebration of life, I feel that my children and I finally found out what happened that night. Euphoria may be an overstatement but there was something we all experienced that evening. It had to be collective effervescence, and its foundation was the love and affection my family, me, and our guests had for our M.L.

CHAPTER ELEVEN

Consider Grieving Through a Magical Celebration of Life

Some thoughts as you reflect on traditional norms and rituals vs. a celebration of life.

- Have the courage not to do the typical or normal thing when someone passes.
- Allow yourself to be vulnerable and share what the deceased meant to you and yours.
- Whatever you do, take some time to consider how you want to have that person who passed honored.
- Allowing yourself some time to grieve and collect yourself before you celebrate can be a good thing.
- By taking the risk of doing something different, people opened up to my family and me more authentically because we were authentic and genuine.
- The heaviness of my M.L.'s loss lightened significantly after the celebration. Her loss will always be with me and yes, the grief felt lighter and *yes,* that celebration was as magical as my M.L.
- Consider doing a real celebration, a party. Do it for your loved one and yourself. It just might be the new normal, grieving your loss through a magical celebration of life.

Thank you for reading this and considering these thoughts.

PART TWO

Poetry: Inspired by my M.L.

That Day

My M.L. completed thirty-three radiation treatments and chemotherapy. The radiation treatments were supposed to be conducted over seven weeks—it took her twelve weeks because of her physical limitations. It was sometimes debilitating to her but she endured it.

Chemotherapy was worse; the medical team kept changing the concoction but M.L.'s body largely rejected all of them. She managed a number of treatments, and ultimately needed to stop.

We headed to Boston's Dana-Farber for a meeting with M.L.'s oncology team. At that meeting they explained that there was nothing else they could for my M.L. There was some discussion about some "less harmful" chemo cocktails but the lead oncologist told us that "M.L. should enjoy her time." He added that he would not recommend the treatment he had just suggested to his sister or wife.

She was characteristically stoic. I was broken.

When we entered our vehicle she said let's go out to eat at a nice restaurant. We did. She insisted we take the picture on the right.

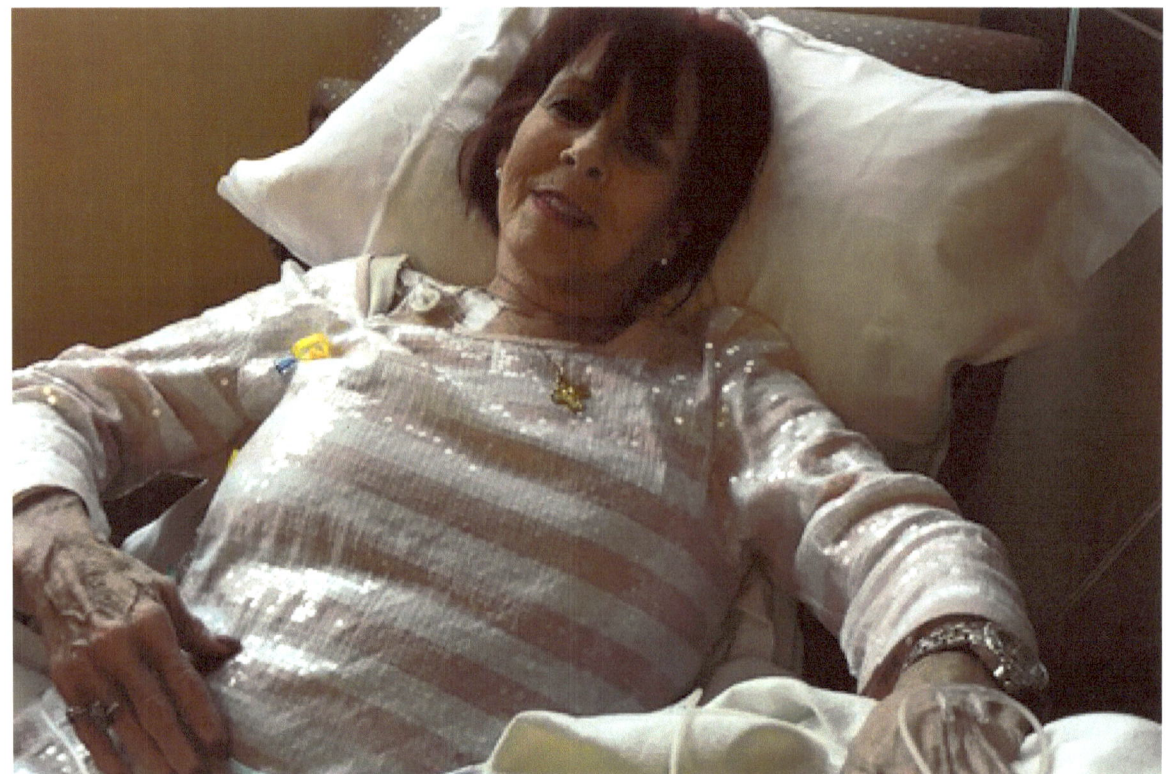

Over the next week or two, as my M.L. napped, I wrote some poems. I felt as though I had been sliced in half. Words seemed to tumble from my heart onto paper.

I gave her the poems; she loved them, embraced me, and thanked me for them. She asked me what I wanted to do with them; I said "Nothing, they're for you." She smiled and said okay.

At a follow-up appointment with her medical team in Rhode Island, my M.L. gave them to her medical oncologist, Dr. Sabrina Witherby. Dr. Witherby could teach a doctorate level course in bedside manner.

Dr. Witherby and one of her assistants said that we should share the poems and that there were online cancer journals that would publish them. Before I could reply, my M.L. had already approved that this was okay with her.

I looked at her quizzically and she said, "You said they were mine, so there you go my love. Let's see if someone wants to publish them."

Later she explained that she thought it might help another couple experiencing similar challenges.

The next thing I knew an online publication called *Cancer Cure* called me, asked me a few questions, and advised me that they would like to publish the poems.

I don't know if they are all that good but they are genuine and I wrote them at a very low point for me. My M.L., on the other hand, just kept living her best life even with all those illnesses that slowly took her from this life.

What follows are the poems as they appeared in *Cancer Cure*. They were published in June of 2019.

Holding Her Smile in His Heart Forever

June 5, 2019

A devoted husband and caregiver shares the poetry he wrote for his beloved wife, Mary Lee, after doctors gave her 18 to 36 months to live.

My name is Guy Marini and I am the caregiver for my wife Mary Lee, whom I lovingly refer to as "my M.L."

My M.L. has multiple sclerosis, end-stage COPD, and stage 4 colorectal cancer that has metastasized to her lungs. She has been given 18 to 36 months to live.

I have been writing some poetry to express my feelings about her/our situation. I have shared these poems with very few. The response has been very positive. I offer them to the *CURE* audience. My hope is that they will help others who are going through similar troubles.

18 TO 36 MONTHS

18 to 36 months they say with eyes downcast
That's how long we expect her to last
They mean well, they are learned but do they know
The force of her mind and the warmth of her glow
18 to 36 months...the words tumble out with sadness
How to go on without constant madness
They look down, study their hands...and wait
She holds my hand, smiles softly...expressing no complaint
18 to 36 months...they mean so well
It's time not to dwell
On treatment, false hope, and regret
Enjoy life, stay strong...while sadness begets
18 to 36 months...they really don't know
The fight in her heart, the strength of her soul...and so
Thank you for the prediction and well-intended words
But for now, she will be one with the birds
That sing outside her window as we enter spring and fly
In search of cloudless sky and bring
Smiles to our faces providing sweet music to our glorious kingdom
As they enjoy freedom
18 to 36 months is a guess that gives her pause
And drives her to push the laws
Of medicine, trite statistics, and the like
As she prepares for a long, tough fight.
For in her is the heart of a tigress
Who amazes in beauty, strength, and kindness
18 to 36 months...the writer doesn't agree
Because he has seen her so beautiful and free
Of worry and care with a deep well of feeling
She is one who keeps me believing
18 to 36 months...just numbers, a guide post...a guess
But not imagined to be true by me or my lovely lioness

HOLDING YOUR SMILE IN MY HEART FOREVER

I will hold your smile in my heart forever.

Forgetting that spark of light...never.

Your soul emerges in its beauty with force.

If I couldn't see it I would be filled with remorse.

Your bright eyes beam, your nose twinkles, and your cheeks bloom.

People look in wonder as you fill the room with your special warmth...joy...and soon.

You look at me with your soft, warm smile and I realize I have fallen for you yet again while my heart is filled with love and admiration.

So, I must keep you with me as your touch overwhelms me like a swirling ocean.

I will hold your smile in my heart forever...

Forgetting your love force...never.

OUR QUANDARY

Sickness ravages her body and not her mind.
Her will is strong and unable to break the bind.
How to live...how to die...how to be?
How to quiet your mind to rest soundly.
Her beauty explodes...her eyes soft and blue.
Her touch softer than a mild spring dew.
I dream that she will be well somehow and the reality makes my head bow.
She lives day by day by simply conserving her strength.
I pray for her recovery and a life vision with breadth.
And she struggles and I love her.
What to do? How to be and wish it were
True that she can recover and thrive.
But for now, I try to help her survive.
Hoping for that smile...that light in her sweet face.
And I feel everything I need to feel in her warm embrace.

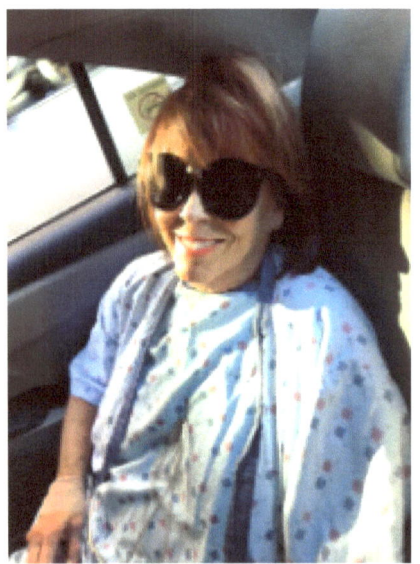

IS THIS WHAT DYING FEELS LIKE?

She asks — "Is this what dying feels like?"
I'm struck by the question.
Her face is sad, somber...eyes no longer bright.
We stare at each other...no answer...only reflection.
"How could I know?" I respond.
"Do you feel weaker...hopeless?"
I wish for that mythical magic wand.
She says..."I'm exhausted, empty, restless.
No energy, motivation, or will to go on."
I tell her — "Your loved ones need you here."
Is that the right thing to say...who knows...it's with us she belongs.
She smiles broadly and tells me she holds me, dear.
What to do but strive to make the best.
I hurt...I've cried...but I don't know how she feels.
Maybe she wants to go to her eternal rest.
Her life force slowly draining while my heart reels.
How does it feel to be dying?
Haunting, loving, surreal, and trying.

DEATH AND BEAUTY

She is slowly dying yet more beautiful than ever.
Her body wilts and she sighs with weakness.
Yet her eyes still sparkle like glowing ember.
And she reaches to embrace me with loving kindness.
Somehow she has a renewed dignity.
While living her life in pure futility,
I cannot fathom her beauty as she fades away.
It's not understandable yet I observe it every day.
Is my heart changing my perception?
Her growing beauty my heart's reflection.
I look for an answer and wonder —
Somehow it feels like our love is more tender...fonder.
Overwhelmed by the future and the too-soon-to-arrive loss.
Is her growing beauty just another one of life's agonizing twists?
Or love's final beautiful, amazing gift.

SWEETNESS AND SADNESS

Sweetness and sadness visit us daily,
There are tears...but, frankly, rarely,
Sadness comes in the way of no energy and sighs,
Sweetness comes with the sparkle in her eyes.
Sweetness and sadness visit us all the time,
At times we forget...know we are lucky...it's sublime,
Then darkness rolls in without warning as she gasps for air.
In the next moment...any dreams of the future are laid bare.
Sweetness and sadness never leave us alone,
Both have their place in our lives and home,
Sadness as her hands tremble and shake,
Sweetness...when another kiss from her I take.
Sweetness and sadness...how does this make sense,
As life goes from joy to being meaningless,
Sweetness...our love continues to grow,
Sadness...we hope the days will pass slow.
Sweetness and sadness...you need to go on,
And work extra hard to be strong,
The sadness is bearable because our hearts are one,
And we know the sweetness will never, ever be over and done.

*Guy Marini, in addition to being his wife's caregiver, writes children's books.
You can visit his website at www.supernonnobooks.com and he invites
readers to connect with him on LinkedIn.*

For my M.L., from Guy.

PART THREE

Ring the Bell for Our M.L.
Helping Children Understand Loss

Ring The Bell For Our M.L.
Helping Children Understand Loss
By Guy Marini

A Super Nonno Book

RING THE BELL FOR OUR M.L.
Helping Children Understand Loss

A Super Nonno Book
By Guy L. Marini

Illustrated by
Tom Arvis

DEDICATION

This book is dedicated to my grandchildren, Ethan and Makenzie Marini. Their talks with me about the passing of their Nonna M.L. provided the inspiration for this book.

Nonna M.L was a loving, cheerful, amazing Grandmother
that Ethan and Kenzie simply called Nonna.

Nonna loved to do arts and crafts with Ethan and Makenzie. Nonna created a room in her home to do arts and crafts with Ethan and Kenzie- they called it " The Imagination Station!!!" They would draw and paint together for hours. Nonna and Makenzie drew flowers and animals while Ethan and Nonna focused on cars, trucks and fire engines.

4

Does anyone like cookies?
Well, Nonna, Ethan and Kenzie loved making and baking sugar cookies especially at Christmas time... Santa cookies, reindeer cookies, snowman cookies... Some sprinkled with different colored sugar - others with Nonna's special vanilla frosting... Give me a glass of cold milk and warm sugar cookies...
PLEASSSSE!!!

Nonna loved her backyard...there was a gazebo filled with flowers...A playhouse for Ethan and Kenzie...a little pond with a waterfall and fish...a hammock for her husband, Nonno Guy and flowers, flowers and more flowers...it was so beautiful - the birds, squirrels, rabbits and chipmunks came to visit all the time.

Nonna, Ethan and Kenzie loved to walk in the backyard in the tall, cool, green grass... Together they would plant the flowers...roses, tulips, lilies...all beautiful...all different colors...after a hard working morning of gardening...Nonna would make a nice lunch that Ethan, Kenzie and Nonna would eat in the gazebo.

Then there was Nonna's beautiful, brass bell...it was hanging on the clubhouse that Ethan and Kenzie played in. It was a shiny, brass bell...when you rang it, it made the most beautiful sound that echoed throughout our neighborhood.

Nonna told Kenzie and Ethan that it was a magical bell. "How do you know it's a magical bell, Nonna?" asked Ethan and Kenzie.

Nonna took Ethan and Kenzie outside and rang the bell. Suddenly, birds, rabbits, chipmunks and squirrels appeared.

10

"Wow! Wow! Wow!" said Ethan and Kenzie.
Nonna said "Oh, when they hear the bell, all the birds and little
animals come to visit and say, in their own way, that they
love us and the yard they get to visit!"
"Well, how cool is that ??!", exclaimed Ethan and Kenzie.

Ethan and Kenzie rushed to tell their Grandfather, Nonno Guy, about all this. Nonno explained that Nonna made all the magic happen...and, her bell, was like her magic wand.

Sometime thereafter Nonna got sick...very sick... Ethan and Kenzie would visit her and bring her flowers and draw with her while she lay in bed. Nonna looked at Nonno, Ethan and Kenzie and said "These are truly blessed and magical times."

One day and it was a sad day, Nonna passed from this life to the next. An angel came and gently took her hand.

We noticed the window was open...Nonna and the Angel waved goodbye and Nonna smiled the most beautiful smile.
Nonno said Nonna went to a place called Heaven where she wouldn't be sick anymore and where she would tend to an even more beautiful garden than the one in Nonna's yard.

Ethan, Kenzie and Nonno were sad and went into the backyard...Nonno lifted Kenzie and then Ethan and they rang Nonna's bell...It sounded so beautiful and clear and sweet...and...sure enough the birds, rabbits, chipmunks and squirrels came to see us.

We were happy to see the birds and little animals but something was different..."Oh No!" shouted Ethan and Kenzie - there was a crack in the bell...it wasn't broken...it didn't fall apart...it was just cracked...we all looked at the bell in stunned silence...

Kenzie and Ethan said - "I feel like my heart is broken and now Nonna's bell is cracked too..."
The three of us sat on the steps, sadly and held hands.

After a while, Nonno got up and rang the bell again - it sounded really nice...a little different than it did before the Angel took Nonna. Slowly, the birds, rabbits, chipmunks and squirrels came back to visit us. The animals seemed confused as they looked at Nonno - It was like they were wondering "Where's Nonna?"...we were all a bit confused...

19

Nonno shared his thoughts with Ethan, Kenzie and the birds,
rabbits, chipmunks and squirrels.
Nonna M.L. was gone from our sight and we couldn't see
her...but, while our hearts seem completely broken apart - our
hearts are simply cracked just like Nonna's bell...

20

Nonno said - "Like Nonna's Bell, your heart is cracked, not broken, and full of love for Nonna and each other."

22

And, one way, we can love and remember our Nonna is to
carefully, lovingly and daily ring her bell.

And when we do...we will smile and remember all the fun we had with Nonna...we will enjoy our friends in nature...the birds, rabbits, chipmunks and squirrels...
And we will cherish the sound of our Nonna's simple, beautiful, melodic Bell.

24

And, finally, over time...our hearts and memories of our Nonna M.L. will be like the bell....strong, vivid, shining and amazing. A little cracked, I guess, but.... The hurt will turn into smiles, laughter and loving stories about our Nonna M.L.

So whenever we go in the backyard we must...
Ring the Bell For our Nonna M.L.

And, yup... when Ethan and Kenzie come to visit at Nonno's house... the first thing they do is rush to the backyard
AND
Ring the Bell for Our M.L.

Nonna M.L. And Her Bell:

Written As A Tribute to....
Mary Lee (M.L.) Marini
January 16, 1957 - February 13, 2020

Super Nonno books always end with a question so that the child and reader can talk a little bit.

Questions to the child:

If you were Ethan or Kenzie, would you feel better by ringing the bell?

If it would make you feel better, please tell me why?

If it wouldn't make you feel better, please tell me why?

If you would like to read other *Super Nonno Books*,
please visit Guy Marini's website:
www.supernonnobooks.com

You may purchase the books from the website or
go to Amazon.com and type ***Guy Marini*** and
the name of the book on the search bar.

Other Super Nonno Books include:
- For the Love of Pizza
- Patsy, Pipi and Duke
- The Boy who Loved Trucks
- Little Miss Excitement
- My Best Buddy M.L.
- For the Love of Freckles
- Super Nonno

Another Super Nonno Book About M.L.:

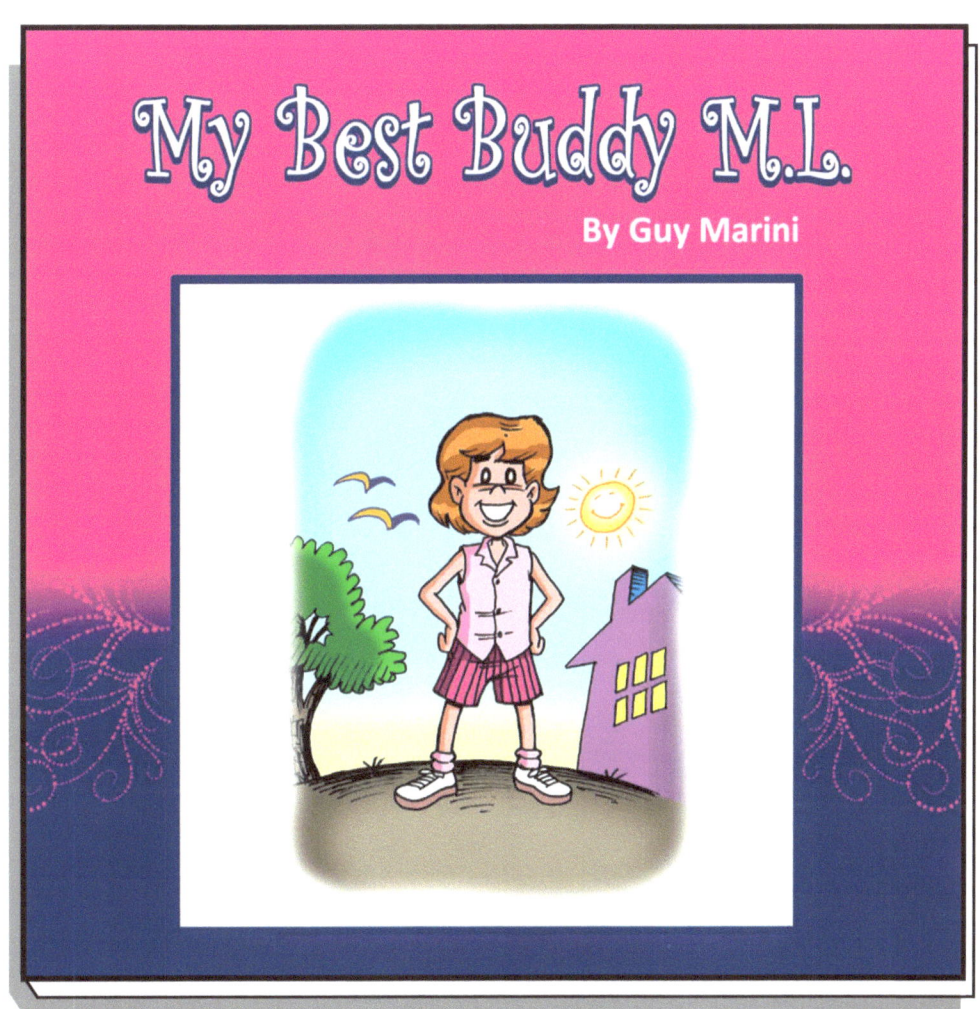

Guy has donated some books to local Hospice Centers
with the hope that this book can somehow help
kids who experience the difficulties of a
loved one passing.

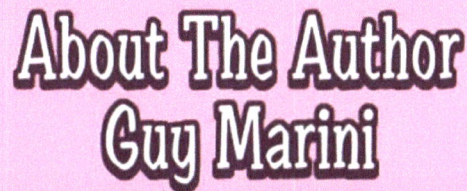

About The Author
Guy Marini

Guy Marini is an author, business man and the World's largest consumer of pizza. Guy lives with his dog, Oliver in Pawtucket, RI. He has three great children and two amazing grandchildren, who motivated the creation of the Super Nonno book series.

Guy is the driving force behind the famous "Marini Easter Egg Hunt" and "Marini Turkey Trot and Turkey Egg Hunt."

Here's what Guy says makes these books different and why he writes them - "Time spent reading to a child rewards the reader and child. Super Nonno books always end with a question to stimulate further discussion between you and the child...Reading time is a sweet and special time not to be missed or rushed."

I was inspired to write this book by my grandchildren Ethan and Mackenzie. At the time of my M.L.'s passing, Ethan was eleven and Kenzie was nine.

Their parents, Matt and Melissa, delivered the news that their beloved Nonna (grandmother in Italian) passed.

Ethan's words, tone, and pain were palpable. "Nonno, I feel like part of me died today." Mackenzie was simply hurting and despondent.

After I talked to them I felt physical and emotional pain. Slowly, they began to talk to me about Nonna, and ultimately their pain softened.

About a year after my M.L. passed, I was playing golf in New Hampshire with my youngest daughter, Erika. We played at a very old golf course in Manchester. As we began to play the back nine, we discovered that the tee boxes from the ninth to the eighteenth hole were dedicated to longtime patrons of the golf course who had passed.

There were wonderful tributes—a bench at one hole, a plaque at another—all with some colorful and warm words.

On one hole, there was a beautiful bell hanging from an old oak tree. A sign asked present-day golfers to ring the bell for old Joe, but only after everyone had teed off successfully to include any Mulligans provided to the hackers.

I looked at the bell, smiled, and said to Erika, I need to put a bell in the backyard with a sign that says "Ring the Bell for our M.L."

Why?

Because my magical M.L. had a vision for our backyard. She transformed it into a beautiful oasis for our family. Flowers everywhere, a small koi fish pond, a gazebo, a playhouse for our kids, a fire table, hammocks, garden Buddhas, wind chimes, the US flag flying, grilling area, discrete/peaceful sitting area—you name it, we had it. My M.L. loved that backyard and in the last couple of years of her life, we spent many delightful evenings there. My M.L. showed Ethan and Kenzie how to plant flowers; they loved it back there.

That's it for context. The book is reprinted here—my grandchildren love the book.

Oh, one last thing: I had an idea for a children's book workshop. I presented the idea to the hospice group, Hope Hospice of Rhode Island, which cared for my M.L. and helped me and my family as well.

I donate the book to kids who have lost a loved one and are part of a Hope Hospice support group. The objective of the workshop is for the kids to write and/or draw their own children's book to honor their loved one who has passed. I share with the kids how I approach writing a children's book and attempt to guide/encourage them. I have started the work of the children's book workshop. The kids are from ages six to fifteen; they are phenomenal, insightful, open, and have given me more than I could ever give them.

My M.L. loved kids and kids loved her; all she ever wanted to be was the best mom and nonna she could be. She accomplished that and I know she approves of the children's book workshop.

A FINAL THANK YOU

Thank you to my wonderful, caring friends and family for their love, support, and for joining the conga line!

One Last Poem

July 29, 2022

On July 29, 2022, I did my first children's book workshop –an amazing and emotional experience.

The venue was created and led by Hope Hospice. The people at Hope Hospice have a two-day camp for young children (ages five to sixteen) who have experienced the loss of a loved one. There is art therapy, music therapy, group time, swimming, games, and yes, in 2022 a children's book workshop.

One of the counselors of Hope Hospice led a poetry workshop for the young teenagers. I decided to attend and be a participant.

Here is the poem I wrote roughly thirty months after my M.L. passed:

NOSTALGIC ACHE

It's always there
It never goes away
Her spirit is somehow alive
She is gone
Her Beauty lives on
Yet I cannot see her
Her presence is all around
Yet there is emptiness
Thoughts of her still bring a smile to my face
And I can't hear her contagious laughter
She lives on in my heart
And it aches so
Yet I know she is here
Still close...still dear
It's been so long without her
Yet I endure the loss
With an endless nostalgic ache
An endless nostalgic ache

Thank you to Roger Clark for introducing me to the words
"Nostalgic Ache," because that's exactly how it feels.